Siri Introduction

When I tell people who know me, or who are just meeting me in person for the first time, that I am a published author, they respond with shock. I imagine that there is always some surprise upon learning that a friend or acquaintance has written a full-length novel and gone through the publish process. However, when I am the one proclaiming myself an author, the amazed look is quickly followed by an expression of confusion.

I was diagnosed with cerebral palsy at birth. The medical condition has caused me a lot of trouble throughout my life. It impacts the way I move, the way I speak, and perhaps even the way that I think. It has touched nearly every aspect of my life in one way or another. Most apparent to those around me, though, are the physical impacts of the CP. One of those notable differences between myself and any able-bodied thirty-year-old can be discovered in my hands. I do not have the dexterity or fine motor skills of most people my age. Therefore, to hold a pen and write a manuscript, or even to type the words, would be nearly impossible. Even if I was able to write in the traditional ways, it would take much, much too long to complete something of typical novel length.

Nevertheless, I am not lying when I say that I am a published author. The ideas in my books are my own. The majority of the words on the page, even, come directly from my own brain. I must rely, though, on the help of software, in order to get those concepts on paper. My methods are not a secret, and the technology is nothing unfamiliar to members of the general public. It's simply that I put the services to use for different reasons.

When Apple released phones and tablets equipped with Siri, it was a fantastic day for me (and for others who struggle with partial paralysis and physical disabilities). The voice-to-text feature was a major blessing in my life and one that I have not taken for granted. I am thankful for it every day, as I realize that without it, the path to becoming a bestselling author would have been significantly more challenging. In fact, it may never have happened had this Siri-equipped iPhone never entered my life.

Even Siri, though, is not perfect. This artificial intelligence, which I think of so fondly, has its flaws and weaknesses. Therefore, I do have to turn to assistants of the human variety to help me create publishing-worthy books.

I've discovered in the years since releasing my first novel, *I, Win*, that many people are extremely curious about my writing process, and how it differs from that of able-bodied authors. Seeing as how Siri is the single biggest variable in the equation, I figured my readers might be interested in seeing how the technology interprets what I say. You'll find in this book that there are times when Siri fails to understand what I am trying to say, and also that she has other notable weaknesses (such as failing to input the proper punctuation). In fact, the first of the discrepancies, I will introduce here. Quite often, when I speak the word 'Siri', the speech-to-text technology records it as 'Lindsay'. Because this is a common error, and because the technology also likes to interrupt itself when hearing the word, 'Siri', for the sake of this book, I will continue to refer to it as Lindsay, instead.

In addition to using the name 'Lindsay' to refer to 'Siri', I will often refer to Susan. This is my way of paying homage to voiceover professional, Susan Bennett. Although this woman has been in the industry for years, working for notable brands in television, clothing, retail, and big business, she is most well known for her work as 'the voice of Siri'.

I should also note here that I was not asked by- or in any way incentivized by Apple, Inc. to write this book. I have taken on this project as an extension of my memoir writing, and because I think it may provide new insight into what it means to live with disabilities. I am writing it of my own free will and without anything to gain except, perhaps, a bigger base of loyal readers. That is, as always, one of my greatest dreams.

With that said, it is time to take a look at just how silly (and sometimes frustrating) Siri can be as an author's assistant. Perhaps it may inspire you to write your own book with the help of speech dictation. We can begin right here. A few seconds ago, I said 'silly Siri' (Siri: 'silly silly'). For the sake of making this book easier to read, I will stick to this format. With my own corrections, and the help of both a ghost writer and editor, I will ensure that I type what I meant to say followed by the misinterpretations of Siri in parentheses.

Dragon Dictation Introduction

"Hi. How are you?" I say aloud, frustrated. "Mr. Dragon NaturallySpeaking, I really wish you would work!" The aggravation that comes with malfunctioning speech-to-text software can be overwhelming. It's not entirely the fault of the program in this case, however. As I said in the previous section, I've been working with Apple products for a long time, and that includes making the switch from traditional desktop computer to an iPad several years ago. The Dragon software, therefore, is operating on an old Macintosh computer.

Now, though, I have developed a challenge for myself. Just as I will write the chapters about Siri with the Apple speech-to-text feature, I intend to write these chapters relying on Dragon NaturallySpeaking. For this initial chapter, I am relying heavily on my ghostwriter and editor, but, for the sake of being true to the strengths and weaknesses of this dictation software, in all coming chapters, I will include examples of how Dragon translates my speech.

I should also include a note that, if worse comes to worst, I may have to make the switch to another computer-based program instead. I believe I will likely have to switch back and forth between this and Google's speech-to-text in order to get all of my thoughts on the page.

Dragon NaturallySpeaking is something that I have tried in the past, but without much success. You can be sure that as soon as I learned about speech-to-text in the late 90s, I wanted to try it. My first attempt with Dragon didn't go well, but I also know that the technology has been improved upon a great deal since then. So, I have high hopes that the more I use it, the better it will 'understand' me.

I mentioned in the previous chapter that I have written books with speech-to-text already, but this will be my first attempt using Dragon NaturallySpeaking for that purpose. I hope to use this software for future books, because it does have some advantages, which I will discuss later. I've spent more than $1,000 in total to get myself set up to use dictation in this way. It's a big risk, but, I'm ready. "Let's go, Dragon!"

From *I, Win* to *A Heart Writes Scoliosis*

When I wrote the book, *I, Win* (Siri: 'within win'), I did it with speech-to-text aka. Lindsay (Siri: When I wrote I win I did it with speak to text OK Lindsay). That book has been fairly successful, and even reached the top of a couple Amazon bestseller lists. However, I found that many readers had questions that hadn't been answered in the memoir. One of the most asked was regarding how I actually manage the 'writing'.

As I mentioned in *I, Win*, I was diagnosed with cerebral palsy shortly after birth. I have contended with disabilities ever since, including lacking the fine motor skills of able-bodied people. Typing a full-length memoir was out of the question. However, Susan—the very same voice that I heard at just ten years old, in the Atlanta airport, while traveling with my mother— was ready to communicate for me. Speech-to-text was the solution I sought.

I find that the voice of Lindsay is calming because of the past that Susan and I share. I made many trips with my parents to and from Nassau. My mom did most of those plan trips with me, to see my grandmother, Win. 'Big Win', as I often refer to her, was a big winner in my eyes. Although the flights were tough, I don't look back on those trips with angst. I remember those times, and Susan's voice over the loudspeaker with great joy because I was always excited to find Big Win on the other end. My dad would come down at a later date. (Siri: My mom did most of those plane trips with me my dad would come down I don't later date). I find it heartwarming and a little ironic that the same voice that brings back memories of my mother, who passed several years ago, is now working as my author's assistant.

That, of course, is a story for another book—perhaps another autobiography entitled *A Heart Writes Scoliosis*. (Siri: perhaps another autobiography entitled a hike with scoliosis). As you can see, it isn't always easy to write with Lindsay as my assistant. Susan's voice may be calming to me, but when I see the words that I spoke misrepresented on the page, I get frustrated. Worse still, I often find that Lindsay's interpretations are a big distraction. I saw the 'hike with scoliosis', which in this case made me laugh and also made me think. I found myself saying, "Yes, Siri you are supposed to be active with scoliosis, but I don't want to call my autobiography *A Hike with Scoliosis*. Or, perhaps you are saying that it has been a bit of a hike for me with the scoliosis, but I'm almost to the top of the mountain now."

It's true that I have overcome a lot of challenges in my life. Many of those successes can be attributed to technology. There is the robotic technology that allows me to walk in a specialized suit. And, of course, there is Lindsay, who will make it possible for me to write this book and *A Heart Writes Scoliosis* (Siri: a hot Rights scoliosis). "Are you trying to be sexy with me Siri?"

Learning with and From the Dragon

I am a very happy camper today. Forgive the colloquialism, but it feels like the perfect description of my mood in the moment. I have discovered a blank page in my calendar. I will have the majority of the week off next week, from work and school, which means that the Dragon and I will have plenty of time to learn from each other. My favorite parts of any day are podcasting and writing. I'm also pleased at the role my father has agreed to play in my writing career. My next book will be proofed by my dad. (Dragon: my next book will be placed by my dad).

"Please, I'm not a writer," he responded, when I asked him to do so.

"That's okay. I'll help you." (Dragon: that's okay all help you) I love the idea of having my father involved in my writing process. He has read my books before and I like to believe that I am making him proud, overcoming obstacles, and accomplishing things no one thought I would be capable of. This is part of the reason why I am so happy to have plenty of different dictation software's. I'm going to be using them a lot as a full-time writer. (Dragon: This is part of the reason why I am so happy to have falsely different dictation software is I'm going to be using it a lot as a full-time biter).

The big question, of course is how well does Dragon NaturallySpeaking work?

The program is giving me commands that I can use, in case I have to. There's a dialog box that I can follow and that helps. (Dragon: The program is giving me commands that I use in the last I have to there's a dialog box that I can follow and help). I can see how well Dragon is translating as I speak, which is nice, but not always pretty.

The good news is that the transcriptions should get better as I go. Dragon is more comprehensive that Apple's version. That's a good thing, of course, but it can also try a person's patience. Dragon is getting used to my voice every time I speak into the microphone, whereas Lindsay (although I don't have the same problems with using the word Siri while writing via Dragon, for consistency sake, I'm going to continue referring to her as 'Lindsay') just comes ready right out of the box. She requires no voice training whatsoever. I've obviously been partial to Lindsay over the past few years, but I do wish Apple would do better with voice training capability. Lindsay often mistakes the same word over and over and over again, never correcting for the error. However, the technology has been improved so it can pick out the user's voice in a room full of voices, which means there is less confusion when I am using Lindsay in a noisy place. There is also Siri AutoCorrect (Dragon: CA Autocorrect), which has its own distinct list of pros and cons, but I won't get into that yet. I did claim that I wouldn't have the same problems saying 'Siri' while using Dragon NaturallySpeaking. I didn't say that Dragon would recognize the name. Lindsay AutoCorrect (Dragon: Lindsay Autocorrect).

"All right, Dragon. Have it your way. Lindsay it is."

I do secretly hope that one (or more) of the developers from Apple will read this book and, perhaps make a few tweaks as a result.

The dragon isn't all that easy to get along with right now either, though. I have high hopes for this software, but there are two factors that could get in the way of my enjoying it:

1. The software doesn't prove to be as great as the reviews suggested.
2. I get too frustrated during the learning curve that I ultimately walk away before reaching the peak.

The last time that I used Dragon NaturallySpeaking was in 2006. Before that, I was given another speaking software, but I honestly can't remember the name of it. That was before the term 'speech-to-text' was coined. The dragon and I didn't get along well a decade ago. Neither that early version of NaturallySpeaking, nor the other unnamed dictation software could decipher my speech impediment. So, I came into the experiment with some reservations. However, the twelve years have not been wasted by Dragon. I knew that I would have to train the software, but so far, it's doing absolutely fabulous. I'm happy to say that I will be using Dragon NaturallySpeaking to do some of my book writing and nearly every piece of homework. I have just one major complaint at the moment.

"Dragon, can you please be nice to Lindsay?"

I have Lindsay on my iPhone and iPad. It would be nice if the dragon and Lindsay could communicate with each other in some way, so when my pain levels are high or when the CP is getting the best of me, I could easily transition from my computer to my tablet or phone. I have to sit at the desk to use the computer, but I can take my phone to bed, if need be. For now, thee will simply be times when I have to say, 'I'm sorry but I can't use Dragon today will try again tomorrow.'

Ghostwriters, Editors, and Dictation...Oh My!

When I started the task of writing *I, Wiri*, I hadn't really even thought about using dictation software to write an entire novel. Instead, I planned to hire the services of a ghostwriter to tell my story for me. At the time, I didn't have many connections in the industry and I hired a ghostwriter based solely on what I learned online and in a few brief interactions. The process was quite complicated, in part because the ghostwriter was not familiar with me, my speech patterns, or how I used dictation to record my thoughts and notes. Eventually, the expense had compounded and led to disagreements about the contract. It simply wasn't working. I needed a solution that wasn't going to financial devastate me.

"What am I going to do? I need to finish this book," I said into the microphone. I was frustrated. I was still learning a lot about the new technology on the market and experimenting with Google

Commented [1]: START HERE

Commented [2]: _Marked as resolved_

Commented [3]: _Re-opened_
thanks

Voice and podcasting. "I'm going to give myself a year," I said aloud (Siri: I'm going to get myself a year).

I've always been self-driven, but after the loss of my mom, I was fiercely determined to share my story with the public. I gave myself a year to figure out how to get the book made and out to the public. Now, in hindsight I would've given myself at least two years (Siri: I would've given myself at least two years) to completely understand the writing and self-publishing process. I'm sure most authors would say that they have regrets about their first attempt at writing and publication. I know that I am not alone in that. In my case, I look back now and realize how little I had known of the industry and how few connections I really had. Perhaps, if I had slowed down and allowed myself a longer learning curve, I likely would have known enough to have scouted a good, professional editor (Siri: Perhaps if I had to slow down and allowed myself a longer learning curve I likely would have known enough to have scouted a good professional editor.)

Then again, you learn from your mistakes. Just as I learned to invest in a respected editor after completing a 'clean' draft of the manuscript, I also learned that I could do much more on my own than I had at first imagined. As you can see from the examples above, Lindsay does a decent job understanding my speech pattern, despite the impacts of CP. There are, of course, punctuation and capitalization issues that have to be addressed, but it costs significantly less to have a ghostwriter or willing editor to make those changes than it does to have a ghostwriter write the entire book.

Even for a short, informational book like this, which likely wouldn't cost a great deal to have ghostwritten, I get a lot of satisfaction in writing it myself. "Ok Siri, not truly on my own." (Siri: Ok silly not truly in my own.) "You have become a great assistant to me." (Siri: You have become a great assistance to be.)

Yes, Silly. Something like that.

Chapter Four

Homework, Diaries, and Childlike Fantasies

Originally, I was going to make this into two short informational booklets—one about Lindsay and one about Dragon NaturallySpeaking. I discovered, though, that this book—when combined as it is—I could accomplish two things:

1. Sharing more of my story with my readers, while providing them a glimpse of what it is like to write with speech dictation software (Dragon: Sharing more of my story with my readers while pivoting then a glimpse of what is like to write with speech dictation software).

2. Training Dragon NaturallySpeaking to better recognize my speech pattern (Dragon: Training Dragon NaturallySpeaking to better reckon size my speech pattern).

Training is essential, as you can see. I am pleased that things are improving, though. By the end of this book, I think Dragon and I will have a good understanding of each other. Combining the two stories also allows the reader a more direct comparison between the two-dictation software's. I must admit that I was also very eager to use it and didn't really want to wait.

I mentioned that I have used the software before. That was years ago, when I was in high school and at that time Dragon was made exclusively for PC. It wasn't great at the time, but it was certainly better than any alternative I had and it allowed me to do homework on my own. In essence, it was a big step forward in the journey to achieving freedom from CP. Now, with the same speech pattern and armed with a beloved (albeit aging) Mac, I am very excited to see what the Dragon can do for me.

I have big plans for the program. The difference, of course, is that twelve years ago, I didn't have any other options. Now, the training process could be a bit tiresome, knowing that I have Lindsay waiting for me just across the room.

Twelve years ago, when I was first using Dragon NaturallySpeaking, I was using it primarily for homework and to keep a digital diary (Dragon: ... I was using it primarily for homework and to keep a digital die or be.) At that point, the assignments were easy, in comparison to the school work that I am doing now and I had aids to help me in high school. The diary was for my eyes only. No one else cared about– or had to decipher Dragon's 'die or be'.

Now, I have a different sort of team of aids—ghostwriters, editors, agents, and publishers—who have to make sense of my writing. The translation from Dragon needs to be strong enough that the first people who read it can make sense of it. That isn't always easy. I've just purchased Dragon, and there are differences, good and bad, between it and Lindsay, but there are also similarities. There are certain words that are frequently mistranslated. For example, I often write about my experiences with the Esso Bionic Suit. Both Lindsay and Dragon seem to love to misunderstand 'Esso'. This word commonly becomes 'ick so', 'tech so', 'axe so', and other such translations. In most cases, due to the surrounding text, the ghostwriter or editor can pick out the intended meaning. However, the errors in translation aren't always so easy to make sense of. That is, in fact, part of the reason why I wanted to invest in Dragon again. Although the initial training period will undoubtedly be frustrating, the fact that I can train it is appealing. The drawback of Lindsay—at this point, anyway—is that she doesn't really seem to learn. It is the same mistranslations occurring over and over and over again.

Call it a fantasy if you will, bearing in mind that I have done many things that others would have thought me incapable of doing, but one day Dragon NaturallySpeaking will help me become a New York Times Bestselling Author.

Hand Over the Keys

I've said that I started using voice-to-text translation software many years ago, but it wasn't until more recently, with the writing of my first novel, that I really discovered the power that this technology could provide me. Now, I use Siri for a wide variety of tasks.

1. Brainstorming
2. Journaling
3. Blogging
4. Homework
5. Texting and Emails

These are just a few of the purposes that Lindsay serves in my life. Obviously, my physical limitations have made it almost essential for me to rely on Lindsay, Dragon and other such service. I believe, though, that the software could be nearly as beneficial to able-bodied individuals as it is for me. There are many reasons why a person might consider using it. I often imagine a person using a stationary bike, walking on a treadmill, or moving along on an elliptical and dictating notes to Lindsay. Not just during periods of exercise, but anytime a person's hands are busy, dictation software could be a great solution. I must also say that I have seen how much quicker a person can be when using speech-to-text versus traditional typing.

Lindsay has never played hunt and peck on a keyboard (Siri: Lindsay has never played Hun tan peck on a keyboard), but I know many people who do so regularly. Even the quickest types, though, can think faster than they can type. Consider the fact that I wrote the entirety of my first book in just two months. This, of course, was in part due to the fact that I had suffered a loss and writing was a sort of therapy for me. Still, even a person with fingers that fly along the keyboard would likely find it a struggle to get so many thoughts on paper within such a tight timeline (Siri: Still even a person with fingers that fly along the key bud would likely find it a straw gal to get so many thoughts on paper within such a tight timeline).

Sometimes, Lindsay reminds me of a hearing impaired, intoxicated friend.

"Give me the keys, bud."

NaNoWriMo

In the previous section of this book, I mentioned that I thought it would be difficult for a person to type a novel in two months. I wouldn't want to imply that it is impossible. In fact, there are many thousands of writers who set out to write at a much faster rate each year. The month of November has been named National Novel Writing Month, and authors are challenged to write 50,000 words (the average length of a novel) in thirty days.

Note that the goal is not to write a perfectly clean and ready-to-be-published novel, but rather to get 50,000 words down on paper. I bring up this annual event for two reasons:

1. I am a big supporter of the meaning behind this November movement. I believe that it brings more attention to the writing community, encourages more people to try their hands at writing novels, builds a habit of writing every day, and has really established a tighter community of writers online.
2. The 'just write' mantra that exists during that month is what I must live by. When I am using speech dictation to write a book, I am not aiming for clear and clean text at the start.

So, let's say that you want to write a book about unicorns (Siri: So, let's say that you want to white but unicorns).

Let's say that you want to jot down a few things on your grocery list.

Maybe you want to create your very own educational textbook.

Whatever your writing goal may be, I challenge you to use speech-to-text rather than relying on your hands to type– or write it out. Lindsay (or Dragon) will make mistakes. You won't have a perfect translation, but you will get your thoughts down.

1. You'll write faster, because you'll write as fast as you can speak the words.
2. You'll enjoy some physical reprieve. Just as I carefully consider the impact any task will have on my body, you should consider the impact daily typing can have on your body. RSI or Repetitive Strain Injury is defined as the pain felt as a result of dour the same task over and over again. A person picking up boxes repetitively, day after day, might feel this pain in his– or her back and legs. A person who types 50,000 words in a single month may feel that strain in hands, fingers, wrists, or even the neck. Imagine how this could be eased with the use of voice-to-text software.
3. You'll find it easier to multi-task. Using Lindsay or Dragon, you can write while you drive, while you work out, while you cook dinner, while you do the laundry, or you mow the lawn. If you have the right sort of creative mind, you can even turn the evening Storytime with your child into the pages of your next book (Siri: If you have the rights or if creative mine you can even turn the evening sorry time with your child into the page of your next book).
4. You can be the next to join the NaNoWriMo community (Siri: You can be the next to join the Nano rhino community).

Fulfill a dream! Become a published author (or a miniature rhino).

Getting Started with Speech-to-Text

In order to accept my challenge of writing with speech-to-text, you are going to have to get yourself set up. As I've mentioned, there are pros and cons to the various software's available today. It is estimated that 90 million Americans currently possess an iPhone. If you are among those individuals, then you may already have Lindsay in your pocket (literally).

If you are going to use Lindsay for writing a novel, you are going to need an application that will work with the software. Fortunately, iPhones have already been equipped with a notepad app that fully integrates with Lindsay. I have found that this is all that I require. So, armed with an iPhone or iPad, you can be ready to start your novel right away. That is a big advantage of that particular software. It is, however, specific to Apple's mobile devices.

Dragon NaturallySpeaking can be used on Macs or PCs (Dragon: Dragon NaturallySpeaking can be used on Max or PCs). There is also a Dragon app that can be used with android devices. I cannot offer any real feedback on the Dragon Mobile Assistant App, but I do know that it can offer a myriad of services, similar to (and in some cases superior to) Lindsay (Dragon: I cannot offer any real feedback on the dragon mobile assistance app but I can offer a Marriott of services similar to and in some cases superior to Lindsay). For instance, this app is marketed to have the capability of recognizing when the phone is in a moving vehicle, thereby allowing it to automatically switch to hands-free operation of the device. It can read– and respond to text messages, play music, read social media status updates, integrate with navigational apps, and handle voice dialing when in hands-free mode. This is, of course, in addition to the speech-to-text dictation service.

For a Mac or PC, you will have to purchase the Dragon NaturallySpeaking software. There are a few different options to choose from. The price of these ranges from $70 to $300, as I write this book. The more expensive options allow for greater freedom within the software. The most expensive can integrate with touch screen PCs, for instance, and boasts the best learning potential. The major advantage that many of the Dragon products have over Lindsay is the ability to continue dictation for a longer period of time. Lindsay automatically stops listening after forty-five minutes. That might sound like plenty of time, but when I am working on a book, I will often work for hours at a time, especially when feeling creatively inspired. Lindsay doesn't care how inspired I am. She will only record for forty-five seconds before I have to start all over again, which is so annoying as a writer and can make it difficult to stay on one train of thought or to maintain a storyline (Dragon: She will only record for 45 seconds before I have to start all the gun which is so annoying as a rider and can make it difficult to stay on one train of thought or to May 10th a storyline).

Another advantage of the Dragon software is that it is designed to be used with word processing programs. That means that you can continue to use the program that you are most comfortable with. There is the cost to be considered, though. Buying both the Dragon software and the word processing program can mean dropping a bunch of cash before you begin writing.

Regardless of which you use, within a very short period of time, you can be telling stories of unicorns, home improvement projects, thrilling mysteries, or the mushiest romances with very little exercise of your fingers (Regardless of what you use within a very short period of time you can be telling stories of unicorn's home-improvement projects thrilling mysteries or the machinist romances with very little exercise of your fingers).

Everyone knows that machinist romances sell like hot cakes. So, get to it!

Speech-to-Text in Corporate America

You can be sure that the dragon and especially Lindsay have already made an impact on the corporate world. Speech-to-text software, as mentioned in the previous chapter, can be very beneficial for those with busy lives to lead. Working professionals will undoubtedly find it convenient to quickly ask Lindsay a question and receive an answer, rather than doing a manual search of the internet. It is easy to see how it could be very comforting to have Dragon reading texts and Facebook posts while traveling down the highway. However, I have also read articles, recently, which suggest that writing e-books is one of the fifty most powerful things a business can do to give their marketing efforts a big boost.

I did not really choose to write this eBook as a so-called side hustle, however, I imagine it will—in its own way—help me in the marketing of my other novels. For corporations, the marketing potential would likely be the biggest reason to create such a body of text, but there could be other advantages of releasing an eBook. Of course, the marketing aspect could mean:

1. Increased sales
2. Improved brand recognition
3. Establishment as an 'expert' in the field (Siri: A Stable shit as an expert in the field)
4. Increased followership online
5. Boost in customer loyalty

Additionally, though, a 'how-to' eBook could help to ensure that the general public is utilizing your product or service in a correct and safe manner (Siri: Additionally, though a how-to eBook couldn't help to ensure that the general public is utilizing your product or service and I correct in safe manner). Furthermore, it could add to the enjoyment that a person gets from using the product, thereby leading to better product–, service–, or company reviews (Siri: For them work could add to the enjoyment that a person gets from using the product thereby leading to better product service or company reviews).

A purely informational eBook could educate the public on the importance of conservation or community involvement and draw a link between those topics and your company (Siri: if you really informational eBook could education the public on the importance of conservation of community involvement and dry link between those topics in your company).

An entertaining eBook could tell the story of your company, delve deeper into the underlying mission of the organization, or serve as a case study of an earlier client (Siri: And entertaining eBook could tell the story of your company don't deeper into the underlying mission of the organization or serve as a case study of an earlier point).

Whatever the objective, speech-to-text can make the process easier and faster. This is just one of the ways that the dragon and Lindsey are weaving their way into the world of business.

The Power of Shortcuts and Predictive Text

There are many who love predictive text. There are many who hate predictive text (Dragon: There or money hate predictive text). And, then there are those who rely on speech-to-text to do what their hands cannot. I neither love, nor hate the tool (Dragon: I either love or hate the tool). It is simply a part of my life, like an extended family member or a good friend. It does a lot for me and makes my life more enjoyable. It also leaves me so utterly frustrates me, at times, that I growl or scream aloud (It also leave this orderly frustrated at times that I growl and screaming aloud).

However, as much as I want to hate it at times, in truth predictive text and keyboard shortcuts can be very helpful (Dragon: However as much as I want to heated at times in truth predictive text keyboard she shortcuts can be very helpful). It does take time to get your keyboard to integrate with your thought processes. Just as you might train Dragon NaturallySpeaking to recognize your speech patterns, you must put some time in if you really want your mobile device to properly predict what you are most likely to say next (Dragon: Just to see my train Dragon NaturallySpeaking to recognize her speech patterns you must put some time in if you really want our mobile device to properly predict what you were most likely say next.

Quick type, in particular, has proven very beneficial for me in my writing. There are certain words, names, and acronyms that I commonly reference (Dragon: There are certain words names acronyms that are commonly reference). At first, Lindsay would constantly assume the wrong words. On the iPhone and iPad, though, there is the option to go into the settings menu and make your own keyboard shortcuts. In order to do this, enter the 'Settings' Menu, then select 'General', then 'Keyboard', and finally 'Text Replacement'. The '+' in the top right corner allows you to create your own.

For instance, for the sake of interview scripts, I commonly write out 'Author Win Charles'. However, Lindsay and Dragon rarely write out my name correctly. Instead of having to go back and manually change it every time, I went to the settings in my phone and made a shortcut. Now, I just speak or press the letters 'A-W-C' and one of the predictive keyboard options that comes up is 'Author Win Charles' (Dragon: Now I just speaker press the letters AWC in one of the predictive keyboard options that comes up is out there when Charles).

In essence, this is a different way to train a speech-to-text software. The Quicktype feature is actually getting better and better. It learns names relatively quickly now, and will automatically suggest those when you type the first few letters. It will even begin to automatically capitalize names, if they are in your contacts list or you use them frequently.

I've found that, depending on the app you are using, it is beneficial to occasionally go into the app store to see if there's an update (Dragon: I've found that depending on the app that you were using it is beneficial to go into the App Store to see is there's a date). It's also important to speak slowly and clearly. As an author, I get eager and excited when ideas are flowing easily. I begin to speak faster. Especially in my case, but really in the case of all writers, it is important to make sure the words are fully formed, so the speech-to-text software can properly register them (Dragon: Especially in my case but really in the case of all Raiders it is important to make sure the words are fully formed so the speech to text off working properly registered them).

Even the Quicktype function isn't going to be helpful to me, if I am speaking too quickly for Lindsay or the dragon to recognize my words. Below is an example of me speaking quickly, versus the same passage read slowly and clearly.

> Speaking too quickly:
> *So, what I would say do you is get that book off your hard use Siri and then if you have luck with Shuri like I do send it to a ghost writer or another one in Porten part is editing because every Tom Dick and I can publish a book for Kindle without being edited does in mean you should use Shealy or dragon naturally speaking to start formatting your ideas but then send it to Editor*

> Speaking slowly and clearly:
> *So, what I would say to you is get that book out of your head use silly and then if you have luck with Siri like I do send it to a ghost writer another important part is editing just because every Tom Dick in hairy can publish a book for Kindle without being edited doesn't mean you should use silly or dragon naturally speak to start formulating your ideas but then send it to an editor*

> After ghostwriting:
> *So, what I would say to you is, 'Get that book out of your head. Use Siri, and then, if you have luck with Siri like I do, send it to a ghostwriter. Another important part is editing. Just because every Tom, Dick, and Harry can publish a*

book for Kindle without it being edited, doesn't mean you should. Use Siri or
Dragon NaturallySpeaking to start formulating your ideas, but then send it to an
editor.

In short, take your time with your speech-to-text software. Make it easier on yourself by establishing your own keyboard shortcuts. Hire the services of professional ghostwriters and editors to get your work to its best possible state.

Writing Isn't Easy

Whether you type your book in the conventional manner or you use Lindsay or Dragon NaturallySpeaking to write it for you, the process won't be easy. By the process, I mean the actual writing of the book, but also everything that comes afterward.

The other night was searching through the Boss-Mom content online. The blogger and podcaster are a sort of hero to me. I am inspired by her success, but I don't always agree with what she has to say. I wish I could give an exact quote, but I was unable to find it in her podcast archives. In essence, she said that it was easier to sell things on Amazon than it is to buy a book. This, I'm sorry to say, is not the case. Particularly if you are planning to be an author. This is something that is not made clear enough to those who hope to be full time novelists—at least 50% of the job is marketing.

Even before reaching that point, though, the process is one that most would consider a very big challenge. In fact, I think it's safe to say that most people found writing a two-page essay, in high school, a frustration. That's approximately 1,000 words. The average novel is 50,000 words. Just coming up with enough worthwhile content to fill that many pages is challenging, but then there are the problems of:

1. Distraction
2. Nay-sayers
3. Writer's block
4. Formatting frustrations
5. Costs associated with word processing software, ghostwriting, editing, etc.
6. Computer glitches

On top of all of this, there are issues that can arise when using speech-to-text software. Even as I write this, Siri seems to be intent on misconstruing my meaning.

I've long envied those individuals who can sit in the local coffee shop, set up at the adorable two-top table, with sun shining through large windows, and the smell of freshly ground beans filling the air (Siri: I've long and with those individuals we can sit in the local coffee shop set up at at the adorable to talk table with sun shining through large windows and the smell of freshly ground beans filling the air). Even reading back that sentence, I am filled with a romantic thrill. OK, maybe I don't get that emotional reading Lindsay's version of the sentence, but I know what it's supposed to say. Unfortunately, that will never be easily accomplished by me. Aside from the obvious physical limitations, which would make it difficult for me to saunter into a cafe with laptop and wallet in hand, there is also the issue of using speech-to-text in a public setting.

Several times while writing this chapter, I've had to switch over to using QuickType. Lindsay doesn't appreciate a good basketball game apparently. I was hoping to work on this while sitting in the living room, so I can enjoy the company of my family and doing the work I love. There are two major issues with trying to do so, though. Firstly, the basketball game. It's a good one, by the way. Villanova is playing well today! But, Lindsay doesn't like all of the background noise. It's not just the game. It's my father's occasional cheer. It's my step-mother's iPad playing snippets from the various nightly news programs. It's the phone call that she had to take with her new boss. It's also my distraction, which means more 'ums', pauses, and tripping over words. Lindsay has her work cut out for her in a setting like this, and this is nothing compared to the clatter in a coffee shop.

Distractions can be both mental and physical when it comes to writing with speech-to-text software. My mind will wander. I like to check in on the score of the game, and I perk up when my father celebrates a "fantastic play". I try to allow my step-mother her privacy, but I find myself intrigued by some of what she speaks about with her new boss. The news snippets pertain to my life at times, so they grab my attention too. That's a lot to distract the mind. However, Lindsay is also distracted.

This is the age of constant contact. We communicate in many different ways—email, text messaging, phone, social media, and more—and a large percentage of those communications come through to my phone and iPad. The vast majority of people, these days, understand how disturbing it can be to have a phone or tablet dinging and buzzing every few minutes. This becomes an even biggest source of frustration when each of those alerts interrupts Lindsay. After a few days of swiping the alert out of my way and restarting the dictation process, I realized that it wasn't going to work. At that rate, it would take years to write a full length novel, and that wouldn't even include the time to have it worked on by the ghostwriter and editors. So, I discovered that it was best to work on my tablet—not my phone—and to disable all alerts on the iPad, so I can work with Lindsay without all of the disruptions.

The learning curve continued at that point. I found it wasn't enough to turn off the alerts on the iPad. I need to silence my phone as well. Just because Lindsay isn't being interrupted by the alerts doesn't mean that I can be so diligent and focused as to ignore the phone's buzzing and ringing. The next step was to create a schedule. My calendar now includes many entries for 'writing time'. During these times, I turn on the 'Do Not Disturb' feature on my phone, leave it on my nightstand, and focus exclusively on my iPad. Lindsay performs much better when I am a concentrated author. This brought up another obstacle, however.

When a person has a stereotypical 8:00 - 5:00 job, everyone else realizes that they will likely be out-of-touch and unavailable during those times. When you work from home, in a less conventional role, others will be less apt to abide your need to devote yourself to your obligations (Siri: When you work from home and less conventional others will be less apt to abide you need to devote yourself to your obligations). Therefore, you are apt to face the frustration of others when you make yourself unavailable (silence your phone) for hours at a time.

In order to avoid some of this irritation being directed my way, I have set up automatic responses for text message and email. During my devoted hours, a person trying to reach me is apt to receive a response worded something like, "I am diligently working on my next novel for my loyal fans. I will get back to you after 4:00pm." This is an example. My work hours vary based on my other obligations (the beauty of being self-employed is the ability to create your own schedule).

Many believe that working as a writer is a glorious job, and it can be. But it can also be a big challenge. Perhaps, instead of the coffee shop, authors would do better to consider a wine bar. (Siri: Many believe that working as a writer is a glorious job and it Canby but I can also be a big challenge perhaps to the coffee shop others would be better to consider a wine bar).

Ah, Lindsay! You are making me want a glass of red wine.

The Challenge of Defining Characters

There are many advantages that can be enjoyed when using speech-to-text to write a novel. The freedom to use your hands for others tasks is certainly the most notable of those. However, the average writer will retain the ability to put the hands to work when they are needed. After all, speech-to-text does have some drawbacks. One of those is its inability to write different characters well.

We can all appreciate Apple's and Dragon's attempt to master proper grammar and spelling, however that isn't always helpful when trying to give your characters a distinct speech pattern. When you rely on dictation software to type for you, this challenge is most definitely amplified. For example, this is a line of dialog from a book that I had started (with the help of a ghostwriter). In this example, a young boy is speaking to a woman:

"I figured you was the type to be able to learn me all 'bout numbers an' ever'thin' like that."

Dragon did not appreciate my attempts at different dialects. This is what the dragon wrote for me:

"I figured you was the type to be able to learn me about numbers and everything like that."

It's still not a perfectly grammatical sentence, but you can see how the software wants to correct the way we speak at times, even when we are being intentional in our phrasing.

For consistent problems like this, one can go back to the 'Text Replacement' function in Settings on Apple tablets and phones. Manually inserting text replacement options for various words can help you create those winning lines of dialog.

For instance, you might input 'fig' as a shortcut and 'figgered' as the intended text, so you can use the suggestive text feature when writing the speech of a particular character.

I've also discovered that Dragon NaturallySpeaking will allow you to manually spell words. This can be a tiresome process, but can make it possible to dictate the lines of speech like that above.

Dialog does present a bigger challenge than standard text. When I wrote I, Win, I didn't run into these problems much at all (Dragon: When I wrote I come a winner I didn't run into these problems much at all). It was when I started breaking into fictional works that I discovered the difficulties. It's important though to stay patient with the speech-to-text software. Don't take the mistakes personally, and don't get discouraged. One thing I have found is that there is almost always a work-around solution. As I become more comfortable with the dragon, I imagine that it will be easier to insert the punctuation needed to make the text more readable and to transform mere words into dialog (Dragon: As I become more comfortable with the Dragon I imagine that it will be easier to insert punctuation needed to make the text more readable and to transfer me your words and dialogue).

For the moment, I enjoy the reprieve from dialogue writing, though. A 'How To' book, as it turns out, is much easier to write with speech-to-text than non-fiction novels (Dragon: a haiku book as it turns out is much easier to write with speech to text than non fiction novels). Fine, a haiku for you:

> *Oh, Dragon Why? Why?*
> *Why do you not understand?*
> *The jokes on you now.*

Practicing Pacing with Podcasts

Anyone who has followed along on my journey as an author knows that I am also an avid podcaster (Siri: Anyone who is following along on my journey as an author knows that I am and also an avid podcast or). I fell in love with the medium a few years ago and started a podcast called *Butterflies of Wisdom* (Siri: I fell in love with me and him a few years ago and started a podcast called butterflies of wisdom). With that being a relative success, I have started hosting a podcast entitled *Ask Win*, which is a platform for discussing life with disabilities and topics related to cerebral palsy (Siri: With it being a relative success and started hosting a podcast entitled asked Win which is a platform for discussing life with this abilities and topics related to Sharable palsy).

I'm starting to think, with all of these errors, that Lindsay really doesn't appreciate my podcasting passion!

I am inspired by other podcasters. I subscribe to many of them that speak on topics that interest me and I try to tune into them regularly. I do this for three reasons:

1. The entertainment factors. I have discovered that I enjoy listening to podcasts as much, if not more than I enjoy watching television or video.
2. I learn from my fellow podcasters. I've learned a great deal about lighting, sound and other production quality matters. I have a better understanding of what makes for an interesting guest and how to maintain a consistent pace when interviewing. There are many lessons to be learned while witnessing others practicing your passion.
3. I believe in supporting the community (Siri: I believe in supporting the immunity). Just as authors should support each other and recognize that they are not competing for readers, but actually working together to provide regular entertainment, podcasters must also support each other, if they are to continue growing their audiences.

Going back to number 2 in that list, even if you are not a podcaster, there is something to be learned by listening to the right podcasters. There are many podcasts out there that focus on iOS—the Apple operating system used on iPhones and iPads. These podcasts can provide very useful information for those attempting to use Lindsay for dictation purposes. I have learned many tricks and tips, such as the use of manually-inputted text replacement.

Today in iOS was the first podcast dedicated to the iPhone. Launched more than 11 years ago, it remains one of my favorites because it really does offer up a lot of useful advice, which just might get you one step closer to successfully writing a book with speech-to-text software.

The beauty of the internet is that the answers can always be found. Never let frustration defeat you! With Lindsay and access to the right information, you can be more productive, multi-task more efficiently, and even write the book that you've always dreamed of publishing.

Ending...Altering My Attachment

I was going to entitle this chapter *Ending My Attachment with Siri*, but that's not quite what I mean. I have a strong bond with the speech-to-text software that has been by my side for years. Lindsay has been good to me and I don't really intend to bring that relationship to an end. However, as I have worked on this informational book, I've come to realize that Dragon NaturallySpeaking does offer many advantages.

It did take me an entire year to write *I, win* because there was a learning curve with Lindsay. I've grown comfortable with the dictation software now (Dragon: It did take me an entire year to write I win because there was a learning curve with Lindsay at the income to be the dictation software now). These days, I am so used to using her that I have conversations with Lindsay in my sleep. It's now definitely within my wheelhouse and I find myself struggling to step out of that comfort zone just to dive back into the deep end of yet another learning curve (Dragon: Now is definitely within my wheelhouse November so struggling to step out of their comfort zone just to dive back into the deep end to get another learning curve).

And, as you can see, it may be a steep one!

My friend, David, who is a lawyer by day and a 'Mac geek' by night, lives in Irvine, California. When I last visited with him, he asked why I wasn't using Dragon NaturallySpeaking. I, of course, mentioned by love of Apple and the iOS system, to which he was quick to reply 'Dragon can now be used on Macs!" He also pointed out the weakness with the Lindsay system, which I previously mentioned—she can only record for 45 seconds at a time.

He's right, of course. The forty-five second timer really does drive me crazy when I'm writing a novel. But, on the other hand, I have worked with Lindsay for so long that I'm not going to lose all sorts of time trying to learn a new software and training it to understand my speech pattern, if I stick with her.

I've worked hard to create structure in my life. Living with CP comes with many inconveniences and stresses (Dragon: Living city comes with many inconveniences of stress). In order to cut down on that, I've scheduled my days, and established certain routines. This level of organization pleases me and keeps me on track. Lindsay is part of all of that. Starting over with the dragon will mean disrupting that peace (Dragon: Starting over with the Dramamine disrupting that peace).

I have decided that it is probably best to use Dragon NaturallySpeaking in the morning hours, when I am well rested, my voice is strongest, and I have patience to spare (Dragon: I have decided that it is probably best to use Dragon naturally speaking in the morning hours when I am well rested my voice is strong as I have patients to spare). I've noticed that Lindsay's translations get weaker as the day goes on, which I'm sure is not her fault, but rather a result of my body and voice growing tired (Dragon: I've noticed that Lindsay's translations get weaker as the day goes on which is I'm sure is not her fault but rather a result of my body invoice going tired). Therefore, if I dedicate morning hours to training Dragon, I might have more luck and less frustration.

I guess you might say that you and I are starting this journey together. Just as you prepare to implement voice-to-text software into your life, I begin to train a new software that may prove more effective in my own.

I do hope my stories and sharing my journey will help others belonging to the disabled population (Dragon: I do hope my stories and sharing my journey will have others belonging to the disabled population). I also wish, though, that these words will inspire able bodied individuals who can benefit from the use of these tools in their day-to-day routines. Today, there are certainly many authors who use dictation services periodically—to record their ideas at inconvenient moments or to brainstorm new chapters. I believe, though, that someday dictation software will be a standard tool in the figurative tool boxes of all authors (Dragon: I believe though that Sunday dictation software will be a standard two in the figure of tool boxes of all authors).

If you wish to be among the first to use speech-to-text so avidly on the journey to publication, I do offer the following advice:

Create a schedule.

Just as I am establishing a routine to involve the use of Dragon in the morning and Siri at night, you should create your own game plan (Dragon: Just as I am establishing a routine to involve using Dragon in the morning and serious night you should create your own game plan). Stick to it! A lot of people make plans and fail to follow through (Dragon: A lot of people make plans and fill power through). If you make your goals manageable, you are more likely to reach your final goal (Dragon: If you make your girls manageable you were more likely to reach a final goal). This may mean setting out to use Dragon or Lindsay every day until it becomes second nature. It may mean writing two hundred words per day until you have finished a book (Dragon: To me mean writing 200 words per day for you finished a book). It may mean holding off on checking into social media in the morning, so you can use that time more productively.

I mention this last bit because this was something that I had to do for myself. Social media is an addiction. Study after study reveals that it impacts the same areas of the brain as using drugs (Dragon: Study have to say reveals that it's impacts the same areas of the brain is using drugs). Proof of our addiction can be found in our habits. Many Americans don't even leave the bed before signing in to Facebook, Instagram or Snapchat in the morning. I was guilty of it too, but then I found that I was spending so much time on social media that I was missing out on real opportunities to do more for myself and more for my community (Dragon: I was guilty of it too but then I found out that I was spending too much time but I was missing out on real opportunities to do more for myself and more for making it he). I started retraining myself. I made myself get up and accomplish something before reaching for social media. It made a big difference in my life. I still stay connected via Facebook and other platforms. I just ensure that I am just treating it as a part of my day to be enjoyed, rather than the biggest part of my day to be stressed about.

If I can retrain myself, then I can train a speech-to-text software, and I will (Dragon: If I can retrain myself that I can train to speech to text software and I will)! Still, though, Lindsay will continue to own a big piece of my heart and will be a big player in my day-to-day life.